SUPER SPORTS STORIES

PRIYA'S PENALTY KICK

by Blake Hoena
illustrated by Christos Skaltsas

GRASSHOPPER

Tools for Parents & Teachers

Grasshopper Books enhance imagination and introduce the earliest readers to fiction with fun storylines and illustrations. The easy-to-read text supports early reading experiences with repetitive sentence patterns and sight words.

Before Reading

- Discuss the cover illustration. What do readers see?
- Look at the glossary together. Discuss the words.

Read the Book

- Read the book to the child, or have him or her read independently.
- "Walk" through the book and look at the illustrations. Who is the main character? What is happening in the story?

After Reading

- Prompt the child to think more. Ask: Priya rises to the challenge when she shoots a penalty kick. Have you ever been faced with a challenge and succeeded? What was the challenge?

Grasshopper Books are published by Jump!
5357 Penn Avenue South
Minneapolis, MN 55419
www.jumplibrary.com

Library of Congress Cataloging-in-Publication Data

Names: Hoena, B. A., author. | Skaltsas, Christos, illustrator.
Title: Priya's penalty kick / by Blake Hoena; illustrated by Christos Skaltsas.
Description: Minneapolis, MN: Jump!, Inc., [2024]
Series: Super sports stories | Includes index.
Audience: Ages 7-10.
Identifiers: LCCN 2022049558 (print)
LCCN 2022049559 (ebook)
ISBN 9798885243940 (hardcover)
ISBN 9798885243957 (paperback)
ISBN 9798885243964 (ebook)
Subjects: CYAC: Self-Confidence–Fiction. | Soccer–Fiction.
LCGFT: Sports fiction. | Readers (Publications)
Classification: LCC PZ7.H67127 Ps 2024 (print)
LCC PZ7.H67127 (ebook)
DDC [Fic] –dc23
LC record available at https://lccn.loc.gov/2022049558
LC ebook record available at https://lccn.loc.gov/2022049559

Editor: Eliza Leahy
Direction and Layout: Anna Peterson
Illustrator: Christos Skaltsas

Printed in the United States of America at Corporate Graphics in North Mankato, Minnesota.

Table of Contents

Taking a Shot

During a soccer game against the Herons, Priya plays midfielder for the Loons. She watches as her teammate Abby steals the soccer ball.

Abby kicks it down the field toward Priya. Priya runs hard toward the ball. She stops it with the side of her foot. Then, she dribbles it down the field.

Priya dribbles past one opponent. She dodges another.

Then, it's just Priya against the goalie.

Behind her, Priya hears her teammate shout, "Take the shot!"

What if I miss? Priya worries.

LOONS
HERONS

Instead of taking the shot, Priya looks to pass to a teammate.

The forwards are better at scoring, she thinks.

Just then, one of the Herons' defenders steals the ball.

Oh no! Priya thinks as the ball moves down the field.

LOONS
HERONS
8

Moments later, the referee blows her whistle. It is halftime.

Priya and her teammates jog off the field. They gather around Coach Raquel.

"Priya, great job moving the ball down the field," Coach says. "But if you have a clear shot at the goal, don't be afraid to take it."

"But what if I miss?" Priya asks.

"That's OK," Veronica, one of the Loons' forwards, says. "But you have to try. I miss shots or get them blocked all the time."

"And what if you score?" Abby asks. "Wouldn't that be great?"

"Yeah," Priya says with a smile.

LOONS
LOONS
LOONS
LOONS
LOONS
8
10
5
6

The Loons get back on the field for the second half. Priya dribbles down the field.

She looks for someone to pass to, but no one is open. When a defender blocks her way, Priya uses a stepover move to get past her.

LOONS
HERONS
3

Priya sees the goalie in front of her. She also sees Veronica running toward the goal. Before Priya can decide what to do, a Herons' defender trips her. Priya falls to the ground.

TWEET! The referee blows her whistle. "Penalty!" she shouts.

HERONS
LOONS
LOONS
HERONS

Uh-oh, Priya thinks. *That means a penalty kick. Now I have to take the shot.*

She sets the ball on the penalty spot in front of the goal.

“You got this!” Veronica shouts.

Priya takes a deep breath. Then she steps forward and kicks the ball.

The ball flies through the air. The goalie dives for it, but it's just out of her reach. It hits the back of the net!

"Goal!" Veronica shouts.

"You scored!" Abby shouts.

I did it! Priya thinks with a smile.

LOONS
10
5
3

Let's Review!

Priya plays midfielder. Take a look at all the soccer positions!

❶ **defenders:** Players who help the goalie protect the goal.
❷ **forwards:** Players who most often score goals.
❸ **goalie:** The player who protects the goal. The goalie is the only player allowed to use their hands.
❹ **midfielders:** Players typically in the middle of the field who help on defense and score goals.

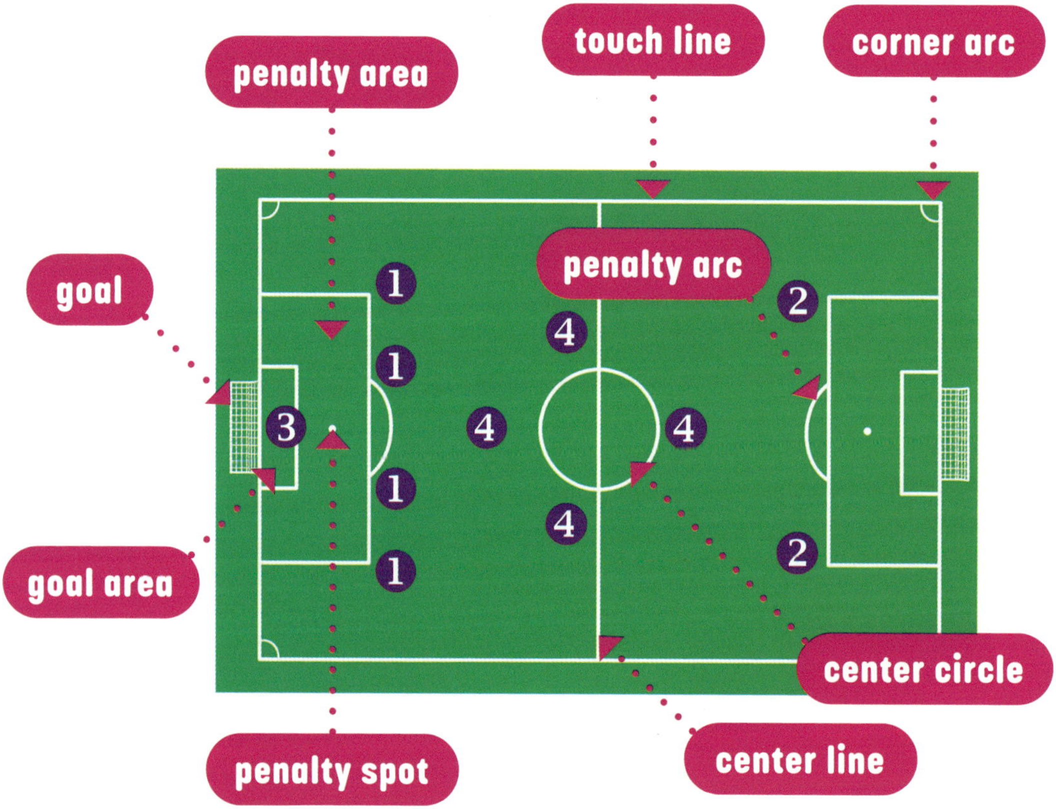

Soccer Equipment

What equipment does Priya need to play soccer? Take a look!

To Learn More

Finding more information is as easy as 1, 2, 3.

1. Go to www.factsurfer.com
2. Enter "**Priya'spenaltykick**" into the search box.
3. Choose your book to see a list of websites.

Glossary

dodges: Avoids something or somebody by moving quickly.

dribbles: Moves a soccer ball while walking or running.

halftime: A short break in the middle of a game.

opponent: The person or team one plays or competes against.

penalty: A foul or unfair act by an opponent that takes place inside the penalty area on a soccer field.

penalty kick: A free kick given to an offensive player who gets fouled in the penalty area on a soccer field.

referee: An official who supervises a sports match or game.

stepover: A move in soccer in which a player steps one way but kicks the ball the opposite way to fake out a defender.

Index